What's Your WHY for Being Healthy?

A Patient's Perspective on the Missing Links to Aging, Disease and Taking Charge of Your Health & Wellness

Carol Van Luik

What's Your WHY for Being Healthy?
© 2025 Carol Van Luik. All Rights Reserved.

No part of this publication may be reproduced, distributed, or transmitted in any form or by any means, including photocopying, recording, or other electronic or mechanical methods, without the prior written permission of the publisher, except in the case of brief quotations embodied in critical reviews and certain other noncommercial uses permitted by copyright law. For permission requests, please contact the author.

Published by Clarity Medicine, LLC | Irving, Texas

ISBN (print): 978-0-9908176-4-2

Printed in the United States of America

MEDICAL DISCLAIMER:

This book and all information provided by Clarity Medicine™ are for informational purposes only. It does not provide medical advice and does not establish a doctor-patient relationship. It is not intended to replace a consultation with an appropriately qualified medical practitioner. You should not rely on this information as a substitute for, nor does it replace, professional medical advice, diagnosis, or treatment. Always consult with a physician or other health-care professional and do not disregard, avoid, or delay obtaining medical or health-related advice because of something you may have read in this book or our website. The use of any information provided here is solely at your own risk. Nothing stated in this publication or posted on our website is intended to be, and must not be taken to be, the practice of medicine or counseling care. Neither Clarity Medicine™, Carol Van Luik, nor any of our sub-contractors can accept responsibility for any loss, damage, or injury that arises from the use of this publication or our website.

CLARITYMEDICINE.COM

Be sure to subscribe to our YouTube Channel: Clarity Medicine

 ## WHAT OTHERS ARE SAYING

What a wonderful look into the amazing journey of Carol Van Luik. This book offers profound insight into areas of my health that no doctor ever identified to me. Giving them the benefit of the doubt, perhaps they never knew. My interest genuinely peaked as I read about microvascular issues. As a Type 2 Diabetic and a Cardiac patient, I realized that my health issues were being managed rather than cured. Carol has spent countless hours and significant resources finding her way through cancer and a host of other health issues. I found nothing that anyone could consider disingenuous or feigned. Instead, I found a forthright and transparent narrative that is both credible and enlightening. I wholeheartedly endorse this book for any serious seeker of an improved level of health and mental clarity.

Philip R. Byler, DRE, DD—
PASTOR, MENTOR | TRINITY CHURCH

What's Your Why for Being Healthy is a compelling, research-driven guide by a passionate non-medical advocate who took health into her own hands. Centered on the critical role of micro-circulation and cellular oxygenation, this book empowers readers with practical, budget-friendly wellness strategies—proving that aging doesn't have to mean decline. It's an inspiring and informative must-read for anyone ready to take control of their health.

Wendy K. Walters—
MOTIVATIONAL SPEAKER, AUTHOR, HEALTH ENTHUSIAST

"So many people spend their health gaining wealth, and then have to spend their wealth to regain their health."

A. J. REB MATERI

Contents

INTRODUCTION	9

Part One
SOME PEOPLE WANT TO KNOW WHY

CHAPTER 1	15
HAVING CANCER OR DEMENTIA IN YOUR FAMILY DOES NOT PREDISPOSE YOU TO THESE DISEASES	
CHAPTER 2	19
SAVING THE WORLD	
CHAPTER 3	23
THE POWER OF REINVENTION	
CHAPTER 4	27
THE MYTH OF AGING	
CHAPTER 5	31
HOW LONG HAS THIS BEEN GOIN' ON?	
CHAPTER 6	35
STRESS & INFLAMMATION	
CHAPTER 7	39
HOW I SCREWED UP	
CHAPTER 8	43
YOU'RE JUST GETTING OLDER – BAH!	
CHAPTER 9	47
RESILIENCE	

| CHAPTER 10 | 51 |

WHEN IMPORTANT INFO IS TOO
LITTLE, TOO LATE (ALMOST)

Part Two — 55

SOME PEOPLE WANT TO KNOW HOW

| CHAPTER 11 | 57 |

CANCER RUNNING THROUGH MY BODY

| CHAPTER 12 | 61 |

SUPERPOWER #1

| CHAPTER 13 | 65 |

SUPERPOWER #2

| CHAPTER 14 | 69 |

SUPERPOWER #3

| CHAPTER 15 | 73 |

SUPERPOWER #4

| CHAPTER 16 | 81 |

GOING OFF THE RAILS

| CHAPTER 17 | 85 |

WIPE OUT!

| CHAPTER 18 | 89 |

OZONE IV THERAPY

| CHAPTER 19 | 93 |

ALPHA LIPOIC ACID IV THERAPY

| CHAPTER 20 | 97 |

EXOSOMES VS. STEM CELL THERAPY

CHAPTER 21 101
  EPIPHANIES—COME AND GET 'EM!

CHAPTER 22 105
  YOUR HOLY GRAIL

REFERENCES 107

IT'S PERSONAL 113
  MEET CAROL VAN LUIK
  PURPOSE OF CLARITY MEDICINE

What's Your WHY for Being Healthy?

INTRODUCTION

We face a significant challenge when it comes to leading healthy, vibrant lives. Stress overload affects our moods, social performance, work environment, and even our sexuality. We will examine health initiatives that have been in place for the past half-century or more, as well as effective therapies being used by an increasing number of physicians and holistic practitioners. The focus will be on repair and maintenance, with the idea that you can also naturally alleviate pain by making repairs.

I became an advocate for my own health when I had cancer in **2016**. Being unwilling to submit to conventional treatment plans that I knew had their own list of formidable side effects, I embarked on a journey to discover what alternatives were available.

What's Your WHY for Being Healthy?

I am delighted to say that I am cancer-free—and I did it without surgery or chemotherapy. I am even MORE delighted to say that through my extensive research, I made incredible discoveries about systemic issues I had previously accepted as "natural aging." What I learned has allowed me to experience improved health, increased energy and mental acuity, lower inflammation, and most importantly, **sustainable** wellness. I no longer believe that getting older means getting sicker, weaker, and more tired. I know this because these are some of the most vibrant, fulfilling years of my life.

Because you are busy, my job is to keep each section brief. Your job is learning to save yourself because being your own superhero is very cool.

The reason for this book is that I found limited information about very effective therapies that were outside the realm of mainstream medicine. It is the culmination of my nine-year search for answers after healing from cancer through alternative health care. I learned that sustainable health boils down to **reformatting our basic beliefs about aging and disease, which we were told were true, and so we believed**. New research says differently. Enclosed are the crib notes from a **73**-year-old patient/student regarding

Introduction

therapies that provided a "factory reset" that vastly exceeded expectations.

I hope what I have learned helps you take charge of your own health and wellness.

To your health,

Carol Van Luik

> *"Wellness is a connection of paths: knowledge and action."*
>
> JOSHUA HOLTZ

Part One

SOME PEOPLE WANT TO KNOW WHY

What's Your WHY for Being Healthy?

CHAPTER 1

HAVING CANCER OR DEMENTIA IN YOUR FAMILY DOES NOT PREDISPOSE YOU TO THESE DISEASES

As I watched my grandmother slowly deteriorate with dementia, I was terrified the same fate might await me. And although there is no cancer in my background, I have dealt with both cancer and the beginning signs of dementia. I was able to reverse both.

Years ago, I was working on development for a Memory Care company specializing in dementia and Alzheimer's patient care. During that time, I attended two annual seminars presented by the Alzheimer's Association and covertly evaluated 35 Memory Care facilities in Dallas and Houston. I learned a great deal, and I was privileged to meet with two experts in the field of Alzheimer's research. One was from the University of North Texas, and the other from the University of Texas Southwestern. Both emphasized that the chance of inheriting a predisposition to these illnesses is about 5%. One also suggested that the possibility might be closer to 1%. So, while genetics can play a role in the development of Alzheimer's, genetics alone is not a definitive predictor.

These individuals also communicated that cancer carries the same degree of predictability. Growing up, I only knew one person with cancer. Now, statistics say that 1 in 3 women will have breast cancer (American Cancer Society, 2024). Over the past 50 years, this dramatic increase suggests that environmental factors and lifestyle changes play a more significant role than genetics alone.

> THE BELIEF THAT WE ARE DOOMED TO GET CANCER OR DEMENTIA BECAUSE OUR PARENTS HAD IT IS A MYTH.

The belief that we are doomed to get cancer or dementia because our parents had it is a myth. The term "predisposition" refers to the fact that we may be more likely to develop certain conditions under specific circumstances. Studies show that only a small percentage of cancers are attributed to inherited genetic mutations, while most are caused by environmental factors and lifestyle choices (et al., 2008; Lichtenstein et al., 2000).

We are predisposed to mimic our parents' lifestyles in terms of diet, activity, and stress management. This conclusion is further reinforced by the study of epigenetics, which reveals how environmental factors can trigger biochemical reactions and alter cellular processes, making us either more vulnerable or better equipped to fight disease.

Call to Action

Be your own superhero and let go of fatalistic beliefs holding you back.

What's Your WHY for Being Healthy?

Family ties do not guarantee disease.

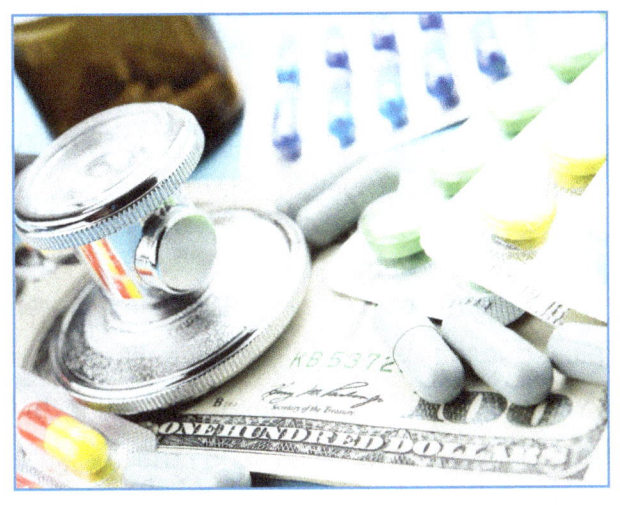

CHAPTER 2

SAVING THE WORLD

Ignoring the red flags regarding health is very costly. I was able to fix the damage from cancer, but in the process, I had to refinance my home. The economic burden of chronic diseases is well-documented, with significant costs attributed to treatment and lost productivity (Bloom et al., 2011).

What if you could save yourself from what we perceive as "normal" everyday illness and pass through the adult stages of life with energy to spare? You can. I do.

During my search, I did not expect to discover a significant loophole in the diagnosis and treatment that is commonly overlooked by the healthcare community. Acknowledging this oversight significantly changes the paradigm of body maintenance and repair and reduces the onslaught of what we consider to be "age-related" diseases.

I healed from cancer in 2017 using alternative therapies, but that was only the beginning of a healing journey to repair stress damage, degrading eyesight, diabetes, heart arrhythmia, and the beginning of dementia … oh, and weight gain! These things appear to be separate issues but are, in fact, connected and will build up over decades until you hit a tipping point. Few people are exempt.

QUESTION

How can the 20,000 miles of blood vessels in your body, of which 90-95% are only one cell wide, so dramatically impact our health?

SHORT ANSWER

Blood vessels can become sick. Poor vascular health can lead to numerous "age-related" diseases by preventing adequate blood flow and nutrient delivery to cells (Celermajer et al., 2012). Sick cells become sick organs (think brain, heart, liver, pancreas, breast, and prostate), and sick organs become sick bodies.

Call to Action

You can be your own superhero and provide your blood vessels with what they need to heal. Research the supplement Endocalyx™, then Ozone IV (intravenous) Therapy, and Alpha Lipoic Acid IV (intravenous) Therapy, which can significantly enhance your body's ability to repair and prevent disease progression (Bocci, 2006; Microvascular Research, 2018).

Sick cells become sick organs (think brain, heart, liver, pancreas, breast, and prostate), and sick organs become sick bodies.

CHAPTER 3

THE POWER OF REINVENTION

In my early 60s, I dealt with severe exhaustion. I had increased cognitive decline, like not remembering where I parked my car and constantly misplacing my keys. Chronic sinus infections that were becoming impervious to antibiotics complicated my situation. I desperately sought answers as my health took a downturn, and I discovered I also had to fight cancer. This is where a normal person asks, "Did you find an oncologist to treat you?"

No. I was not satisfied with the options provided to me by allopathic medicine, so the right choice for me was to embark on the alternative medicine route. My reasons for this choice were:

1.) SIMPLE HONESTY

Several years before I contracted cancer, I had asked a well-respected oncologist how he healed cancer. After clearing his throat, he responded, "Well, we don't heal cancer. Either chemo gets them, or the cancer does." Gulp ... his lack of hopeful options stimulated me to explore alternatives (Smith, 2000).

2.) PAIN MANAGEMENT

I have watched friends die slow, painful deaths on chemo and radiation. Many of my friends assume that physicians can stop the pain. They cannot. Some were able to help manage some of the pain, but cancer is painful. (Haller et al., 2010).

3.) COST OF TREATMENT

I have seen the cost of specialized pain pills to be as much as $16,000.00 for one pill (and that was 10 years ago). I wonder what the co-pay is on that now? The financial burden of cancer treatments can be immense (American Cancer Society, 2023).

4.) INSURANCE CHALLENGE

I noted that an insurance company denied payment for a friend with cancer, which further solidified my decision to seek alternative treatments (Pollitz et al., 2016).

Call to Action

I am sure I could have prevented my health debacle had I known then what I know now, but if you are faced with a cancer diagnosis, do not trust others to handle your medical affairs. Studies show that patient empowerment and involvement in treatment decisions lead to better health outcomes (Hibbard et al., 2004).

Patient empowerment and involvement in treatment decisions lead to better health outcomes.

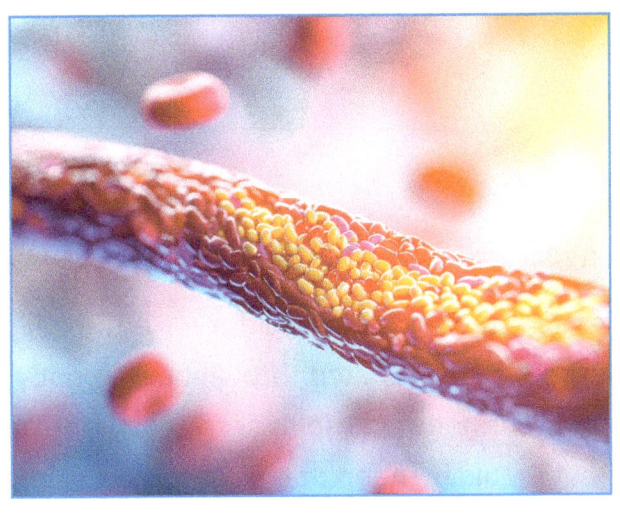

CHAPTER 4

THE MYTH OF AGING

One doctor to whom I paid attention talked about "Zombie Cells" that block the pancreas, causing diabetes. Another doctor spoke about how insulin receptors in the bloodstream were being clogged, so they couldn't accurately assess sugar levels, and yet others warned of damage caused by oxidative stress. In layman's terms, oxidative stress is a form of litter. The common denominator in this equation here is litter! So, let's start with this litter.

OXIDATIVE STRESS

What is Oxidative Stress anyway?! Nobody had ever explained it well to me, but this is what I have learned:

Oxidative stress is basically litter—it is the buildup of waste products distributed throughout the body when the stress hormone cortisol is secreted during anxiety. Perhaps I should mention that anxiety seems to be non-stop for many people. Non-stop cortisol production—that's non-stop litter production!

Prolonged oxidative stress contributes to chronic inflammation, which, in turn, is linked to numerous diseases (Sies, 1997). That and other types of leftover debris get stuck and contribute to what we know as pain over time. Pain is a sign of resistance and a warning that something is amiss. Debris can press on nerves, causing fibromyalgia. It can build up along the spine, causing arthritis. Or it can build up along the brain-blood barrier, causing brain fog and contributing to dementia. Cleaning up cellular debris can significantly improve health, as evidenced by studies showing the benefits of antioxidants in reducing oxidative stress (Nimse & Pal, 2015).

Pharmaceutical companies specialize in a wide assortment of drugs to treat symptoms, and nutraceutical companies have pills and injections to support every issue and tissue in your body. I likely bought half of them. However, these interventions work slowly due to poor vascular health. Healthy blood vessels are essential for delivering oxygen, water, and nutrients to cells while removing waste (Luscher, 1990).

Call to Action

Check your small blood vessels. Improving vascular health through therapies like Alpha Lipoic Acid and Ozone IV can enhance the body's ability to function optimally. Research supports the effectiveness of these therapies. (Packer, 1998; Bocci, 2006).

Healthy blood vessels are essential for delivering oxygen, water, and nutrients to cells while removing waste.

CHAPTER 5

HOW LONG HAS THIS BEEN GOIN' ON?

At age 37, I visited my physician and asked, "Why don't I feel well? I don't have any energy... I'm exhausted... I can't think straight ..."

He responded with a smirk. "You're just getting older." Not much encouragement there. Here are the talking points that I would have appreciated.

STRESS

"Look, there are multiple reasons for what you're feeling. Are you stressed? Stress can make you tired and cause brain fog. Are you adequately hydrated? Research shows that chronic stress and dehydration can significantly impair cognitive function." (McEwen, 1998; Popkin et al., 2010).

BLOOD VESSELS

Did you know that your body consists of approximately 20,000 miles of blood vessels and that 90-95% are only one cell wide? (Yes, I shared that fact earlier—I wish I had known back then.) Constant stress can cause blood vessels to constrict, and if you are dehydrated, your blood can thicken and reduce to slow-moving sludge. This can impair nutrient and oxygen delivery to cells, causing fatigue and brain fog (Celermajer et al., 2012).

EXERCISE AND HYDRATION

Cardio exercise strengthens your heart muscle and allows blood vessels to move blood more efficiently. Adding water is like a rushing stream picking up debris along the way as it filters through the liver and flushes through the kidneys. Regular exercise (weights) and hydration further help squeeze debris through the lymphatic system. (Booth et al., 2012; Armstrong et al., 2016).

LACK OF EXERCISE AND HYDRATION

Lack of cardio and water can reduce lymph and blood flow. It can also impair your body's ability to oxygenate, feed, and wash cells. The first signs of impairment may be cold hands and feet and not sweating during exercise.

What actions might I have taken at 40 if I had known this information?

Later, when my favorite physician challenged me to take control of my health, I said something silly like, "That's why I've got you!" Unfortunately, she passed unexpectedly. Not good.

Call to Action

Exercise—cardio and weight training. Drink water. Pure, filtered water from glass or stainless-steel containers. You'll thank yourself later. A proactive health style (exercise, hydration, reduced stress) can improve quality of life (Warburton et al., 2006).

CHAPTER 6

STRESS & INFLAMMATION

Now is the time to have that "Stress Kills" Conversation. This is a little tricky, because I am still a bit of a stress junkie. Why? Because I get a lot of work done when I'm cruising on adrenaline. This, however, is an extremely dangerous life choice, something I discovered because it works great ... until it doesn't. When it stops working, no amount of willpower will get you over the next hurdle. Has it happened to you yet? I see it show up in many during their 40s and 50s, then blow up in their 60s and 70s. No joke.

Stress response starts in the adrenal glands and pairs with the amygdala to escalate and accelerate your response. When triggered, the brain reacts with an instant demand—"Fight? Flight? Or Freeze?" Chronic stress keeps the adrenals on high alert, eventually leading to adrenal fatigue and exhaustion (McEwen, 1998). This exhaustion, called Adrenal Fatigue, is often overlooked by physicians until it shows up in bloodwork as seriously depleted cortisol levels. Adrenal Fatigue is generally not taught in Medical School, so you must remember to have your cortisol levels monitored. I request a "female hormone panel" with bloodwork to check hormones and cortisol (See attached Stress Model, Chapter 12).

Inflammation, the hidden killer of ongoing stress, is oxidative damage caused by cortisol-related chemical reactions, leaving debris throughout the body. Chronic inflammation can damage tissues and organs, leading to long-term health issues (Hotamisligil, 2006). It contributes to many autoimmune diseases when left unmanaged. Even cancer. (Chrousos, 2009).

Stress & Inflammation

Call to Action

Manage inflammation. Research indicates that managing stress effectively can significantly reduce the risk of chronic disease (Kudielka & Kirschbaum, 2005). Under a physician's care, therapies such as Ozonetherapy can help reduce oxidative stress and inflammation, improving health (Bocci, 2006).

Chronic stress keeps the adrenals on high alert, eventually leading to adrenal fatigue and exhaustion.

C H A P T E R 7

HOW I SCREWED UP

As I rounded this middle-aged curve in life, things began to change almost imperceptibly. My mind became foggy, my vision deteriorated, and the four and five-mile brisk walks slowed to three-mile strolls. I couldn't catch my breath. I felt increasing pressure in the middle of my back against my spine. My heartbeat became irregular, and my blood pressure dropped from 120/80 to 110/70. That's good, right?

Well, not so much!

SCREW UP #1—

I believed doctors when they told me that a blood pressure of 110/70 reaffirmed my health due to my "athletic" lifestyle. This assumption is programmed into most physicians. However, it didn't account for underlying issues like vascular blockage. Atherosclerosis and arteriosclerosis can significantly impact blood flow, leading to heart problems even in seemingly healthy individuals (Ross, 1999).

SCREW UP #2—

I was very active and assumed that I was still invincible. That wasn't very smart. Now I know that visual changes and exhaustion in the early 50s can be early signs of cardiovascular disease. Research demonstrates that early detection and treatment of vascular diseases can prevent severe complications (Libby, 2002).

SCREW UP #3—

I thought I was too young to see a cardiologist. I am not a fan of statins, a commonly prescribed drug for high cholesterol. Statins pull lipids out of muscles (the heart is a muscle), possibly setting a person up for heart issues down the road. Your brain also needs fat to function correctly. According to the NIH National Library of

Medicine, cholesterol makes up only about 2% of our body weight. But when you consider that about 20% of our total cholesterol resides in the myelin sheath in our brain—the fatty insulating layer around nerve fibers that is crucial for the efficient transmission of electrical signals in the brain—the negative consequences of statin drugs are easy to deduce.

I finally did find a physician who understood how to clean blood vessels. Atherosclerosis, arteriosclerosis, and atheroma (benign blood vessel tumors) compete for space along the walls of our blood vessels. This is a very common issue.

Call to Action

Think long game. Checking for plaque buildup in capillaries is the first step toward cardiovascular health. Ozone and Alpha Lipoic IV therapies can assist in maintaining vascular health by reducing oxidative stress and improving blood flow (Packer, 1998; Bocci, 2006).

What's Your WHY for Being Healthy?

"Keep your vitality.
A life without health is
like a river
without water."

MAXIME LAGACÉ

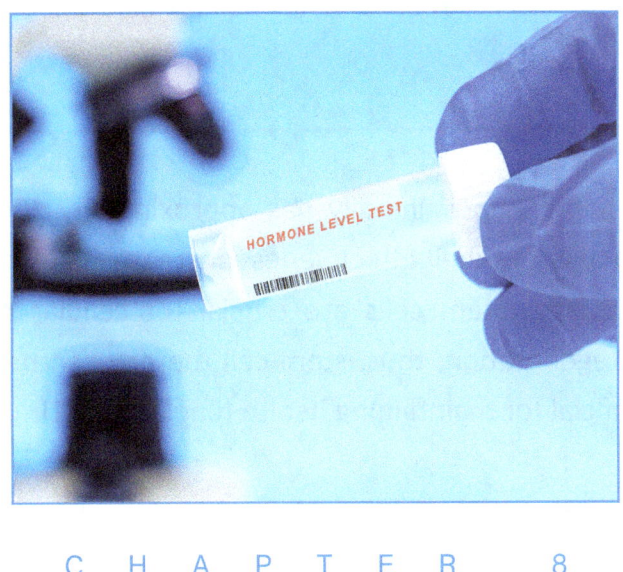

CHAPTER 8

YOU'RE JUST GETTING OLDER - BAH!

Let's examine some bodily functions that degrade over time and adversely affect performance, but are often taken for granted.

DIGESTIVE ENZYMES—

Digestive Enzyme production diminishes by approximately 50% as we near age 40. This means that food may not be fully digested, thus reducing nutritional assimilation on a cellular level. (Meyer & Castell, 1981). Augmenting food intake with digestive enzymes, fresh lemon juice, or apple cider vinegar can aid digestion.

STEM CELLS—

The human body initially has approximately 100,000 stem cells, but their effectiveness decreases significantly as we age. Stem cells are crucial for cellular repair and regeneration; thus, stem cell therapy can be very beneficial for maintaining health (Caplan, 1991).

HORMONES—

Hormones, particularly testosterone and estrogen, play significant roles in how we feel. Stress depletes these hormones as the adrenal glands shift from producing testosterone and estrogen to producing cortisol. Cortisol has been shown to impact heart health and overall well-being adversely (Kirschbaum et al., 1999). Hormones play key roles in mood, behavior, and performance. Standard blood work should include a hormone panel for both females and males. My choice has been to use bio-identical hormone supplementation.

PERIMENOPAUSE HEART PALPITATIONS AND SENIOR ARRHYTHMIA—

Heart palpitations at midlife and heart palpitations as a senior can feel the same, but are derived from different sources. For instance, reduced estrogen can be a source of palpitations at midlife. An irregular beat in seniors may be due to capillary blockage and reduced mineral delivery to the heart muscle. This impairs the heart's mini-nervous system, which comprises approximately 40,000 dendrites (bio-information receptors), from efficiently orchestrating muscle contractions as the heart pumps blood.

Call to Action

Monitor your hormones. Request a hormone panel as part of your annual bloodwork to check to include your cortisol levels. These levels serve as key indicators of hormone deficiency and elevated cortisol levels. Bio-identical hormone replacement therapy can be beneficial in addressing hormonal imbalances (Lobo, 2008). This therapy can be a great help in maintaining hormone imbalances and the management of stress.

> *"Half the costs of illness are wasted on conditions that could be prevented."*
>
> DR. JOSEPH PIZZORNO

CHAPTER 9

RESILIENCE

Is professional healthcare counting on us being sick? You decide. Treating sickness without providing cures is a profitable business model and a massive revenue generator. Do you want to participate? It's your choice! In the expansive use of pharmaceuticals and nutraceuticals (nutritional and dietary supplements), we are the overly trusting patients who allow others to decide for us. It is time for you to take back your power!

Proactive health management means that you must seek out the physicians who "wear the white hat," ... like the good guys in the old westerns, you know, prioritizing your health over their profit. Researching and seeking out healthcare providers focusing on prevention and holistic health can significantly improve outcomes (Berwick, 2009).

If you're in your 50s, it's time to pay attention now! Small, minor symptoms soon become massive, problematic symptoms without intervention. They don't just go away. Regardless of the treatment, they persist unless you commit to a systemic cleansing.

Regular cleansing to remove toxins and improve vascular health can help prevent the cascade of symptoms that lead to severe health issues. Studies show that detoxification and improving blood vessel health can significantly enhance overall well-being (Genuis, 2011).

In retrospect, I wish I had started cleansing my body sooner, but I was too cheap. Therein lies the joke. Prevention costs a lot less than breaking and trying to fix. The downward spiral begins with little things, like weight gain, fatigue, brain fog, and insulin resistance (pre-diabetes). In time, these take a hard turn, evolving into things like diabetes, heart disease, and cancer. *Ouch!*

Call to Action

Learn about therapies like Alpha Lipoic Acid IV and Ozone IV. These can provide effective ways to remove inflammation, repair blood vessels, and contribute to sustainable health and resilience (Packer, 1998; Bocci, 2006).

Regular cleansing to remove toxins and improve vascular health can help prevent the cascade of symptoms that lead to severe health issues.

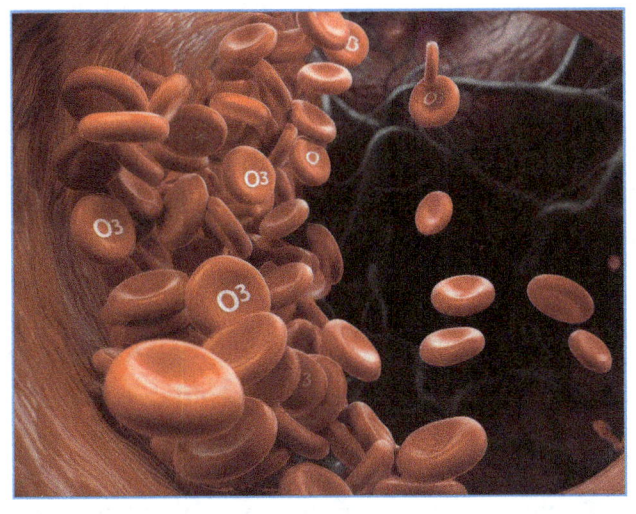

CHAPTER 10

WHEN IMPORTANT INFO IS TOO LITTLE, TOO LATE (ALMOST)

Let me tell you why I started searching for Oxygen Therapy. While traveling in upstate New York, I passed an Oxygen Bar years ago. I was travel-weary and wondered if an O2 hit would give me a noticeable energy boost. It did. ENERGY! MENTAL CLARITY! WOW! I returned to Texas and immediately googled "Oxygen Bars in Texas." Zero. They were illegal.

Nowhere was there a correlation between Oxygen Therapy and Ozone Therapy. Had I known about Ozone Therapy, these past 10 years would have been vastly different. Despite the benefits, accessing such therapies has been challenging. Regulatory restrictions, limited availability, and high costs made them somewhat prohibitive. Still, you should proactively gather information and find providers who offer these treatments. It's important. (Fitzgerald et al., 2010).

Finally, I jumped ahead to new products and therapies. Why? Because I was running out of time. While Big Pharma spends millions on research, it focuses on patentable products that fit the health insurance model. Nutraceutical companies spend far less on research in my opinion, and this is a concern. I needed to know how to spend my resources wisely, so I worked through trial and error, taking notes to document my results.

I enjoy reading medical abstracts and following new research in my spare time. (How sick is that!?) So, the idea of using a therapy that delivered oxygen made sense. More recently, Oxygen Therapy, including Ozone Therapy, has been shown to improve energy levels and mental clarity by increasing oxygen delivery to tissues and enhancing cellular function (Bocci, 2006).

After using Ozone Therapy for two years, it earned its place in my short list of recommended therapeutics.

Ozone IV Therapy was a significant development for me because it became clear that the quality of our internal delivery system has a substantial impact on the effectiveness of any substance introduced into the body.

It is noteworthy that many people's first response after hearing about a new therapy is to consult their physician. That makes total common sense. I have noticed, however, that it is quite standard, perhaps due to our human nature, that a person accepted as an authority (such as a physician) often negates an answer to a question or a solution that falls outside their purview. No one likes to admit ignorance.

Call to Action

No one has all the truth. You must search for it and keep searching until you find the answer. Ultimately, you are responsible for your own health. Even if you abdicate decisions, the consequences to your health are yours alone to bear.

What's Your WHY for Being Healthy?

> *"The higher your energy level, the more efficient your body. The more efficient your body, the better you feel and the more you will use your talent to produce outstanding results."*
> — TONY ROBBINS

Part Two

SOME PEOPLE WANT TO KNOW HOW

What's Your WHY for Being Healthy?

CHAPTER 11

CANCER RUNNING THROUGH MY BODY

Statistics show an alarming increase in the number of women who will experience breast cancer. I never thought one would be me—the quintessential poster child for senior wellness. Truthfully, I only knew one person with cancer when I was young. Notably, the increase in the incidence of cancer does not point to genetics but to lifestyle and environment.

Being a cancer patient and a survivor was not on my radar. Being someone who conquered a virus was. After all, it was just a virus, a little bug, and we kill bugs all the time. This mindset proved to be invaluable.

There had always been whispers about people beating cancer alternatively. I knew three who had, and I was sure it could be done again. I have seen patients suffer miserably from chemotherapy, and I knew I couldn't do it.

The question slowly formulated for me. Were cancer protocols evolving to change the "host" so "the bug" could no longer thrive in my body? It seemed utterly logical to change the host, which became part of my strategy. No sugar! Everyone knows that cancer loves sugar (incidentally, my A1c improved as I made this change). My body was very acidic. I strictly kept to the diet (listed below) to rebalance my body. One healthcare friend derided me for being afraid of a "little chemo," only to later comment on the devastating effect chemo had on the lining of his wife's blood vessels.

THERAPIES AND NUTRITIONAL CHANGES I USED TO BEAT BREAST CANCER—

1. Lymphatic Cleansing and Ozone Therapy: 4X per week for 6 weeks (I worked slightly less than my normal hours, then completed these therapies and went home to sleep and heal.)
2. Filtered Water: (10) 8-oz. Glasses Daily.

3. Raw Vegetable Juice: 5 Carrots, 5 Celery Sticks, 1 Cucumber, Bunch of Parsley, ½" Slice of Ginger. Freshly Made Daily.

4. Wheat Grass Shots: 2-4 oz. Fresh Pressed Daily.

5. Ginger Shots: 4 oz. Fresh Ginger Juice Pressed Daily. (with a fresh orange juice chaser).

Why fresh? Because enzymes in fruits and vegetables are altered by heat, and I wanted every possible nutritional advantage. During therapy, I felt the best I had felt in a very long time. My exhaustion lifted, my mental clarity improved, and, of all things, my business increased! Not bad considering...

I experienced no pain during the cancer die-off. By week three, both tumor casings had softened and become thinner. Twice, I experienced a detaching of something that felt like a web-like film shrinking under the skin from elbow to armpit. Those were quite scary but also interesting. That cancer was farther along than I had anticipated. My left breast sometimes had little "implosions" (movements). These corresponded to areas where two solid masses were located.

Thankfully, this chapter of my life is now in the rear-view mirror. I am careful with my lifestyle and thankful for the fantastic support from healthcare professionals and good friends who have been down this road and were gracious enough to help me.

After about a year, my energy started degrading, and I feared the "Big C" was returning. This compelled me to do more research so that I could discover how we created a cancer "die-off" and what I now needed to do to establish sustainable health.

I was encouraged to continue monthly lymphatic therapy post-healing, which made no sense until, like little ducks all lining up in a row, I understood. More and more, the healing improvements involved lymphatic circulation and blood flow. I had not expected that. It took until 2024 before all the pieces came together.

Call to Action

Explore Nutritional and Integrative Therapies. These can provide additional support during cancer treatment. Ensuring adequate hydration, incorporating raw vegetable juices, and utilizing therapies such as Ozone Therapy can also enhance the body's healing capacity (Bocci, 2006; Richardson et al., 2004).

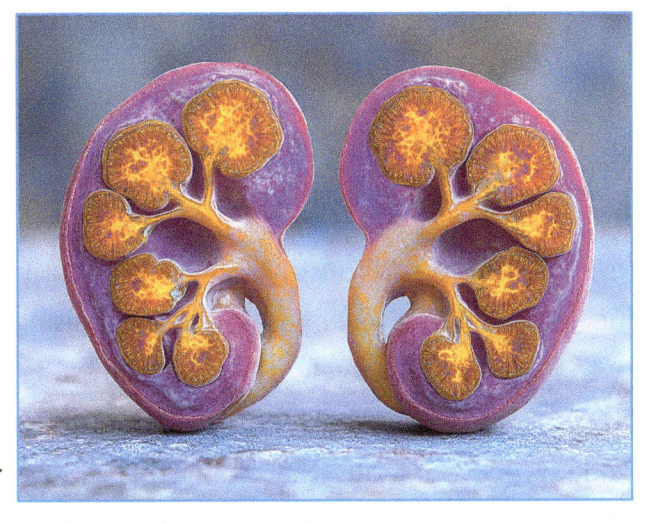

CHAPTER 12

SUPERPOWER #1

HOW I USED OZONE IV THERAPY TO BEAT INFLAMMATION, PLAQUE, AND BENIGN BLOOD VESSEL TUMORS PLUS GAIN A LITTLE ENERGY KICK—

Let's look at your adrenal glands—those two little powerhouses above your kidneys! Their normal function is to convert DHEA (dehydroepiandrosterone) to estrogen and testosterone, supporting libido, thyroid function, and memory coding. Insufficient DHEA may be why you experience memory glitches when you are extremely stressed for an extended period. As stress increases, the adrenal glands reduce healthy hormone production and release cortisol and the biochemical trigger for fight, flight, or fright. *(See Stress Model following.)*

Stress will dump residue throughout the body. This residue accumulates over time, compromising our ability to function effectively. The residue results from Oxidative Stress (an imbalance of free radicals and antioxidants in your body that leads to cell damage), causing inflammation. This residue causes us to appear older, which is generally accepted as a sign of aging. However, much of this is caused by the buildup of debris that invades our bodies. The cool thing is that the buildup of debris can be unbuilt—obliterated. I found it to be reversible.

I received Ozone Therapy (O3) in a chamber during cancer and later Ozone Porphyrin IV Therapy (O4) for two years to remove inflammation. It reduced the pain in my lower back, improved brain function and memory, and gave me more energy. Many patients I know do this therapy monthly to clear out the cobwebs.

ORIGINAL BLOG NOTES FROM 2021:

BREAKTHROUGH: I had been fighting to rebuild my immune system for several years and was still not satisfied until I began weekly rounds of Ozone Porphyrin IV Therapy.

I came to realize that my body was still sluggish—and maybe the reason cancer took hold in the first place was that my blood vessels were packed with plaque and little tumors along the vascular walls, preventing oxygen from getting in and waste from leaving the cells. This therapy is also known as one type of chelation.

I did experience a mental and energy boost once I got past the first couple of IVs.

CONCLUSION: I learned that if there is sludge (residue) in the circulatory system, you are wasting money on any diet, drug, nutrient, or treatment that relies on the circulatory system. It is imperative to fix the circulatory system!

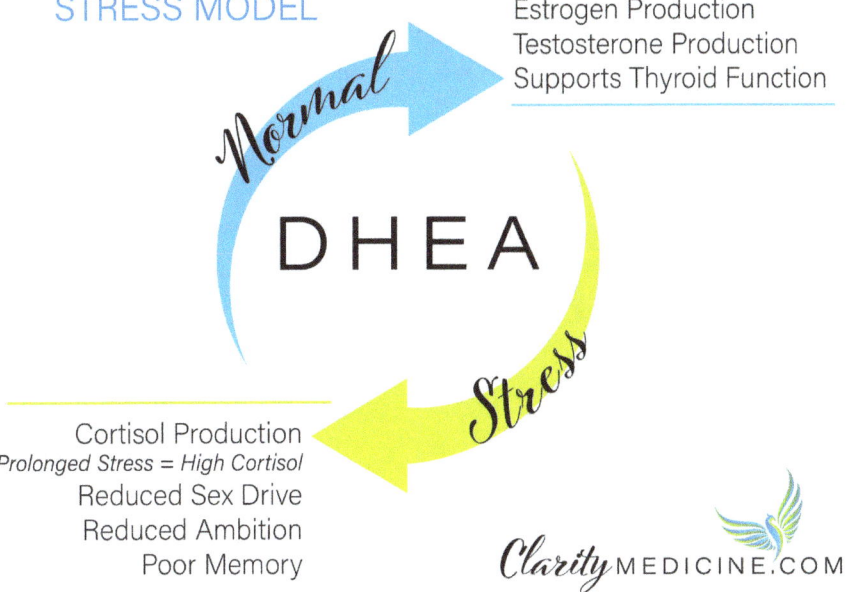

Call to Action

In case you're interested, check out the American Academy of Ozone Therapy website (www.AAOT.US) where you can do a physician search to find someone in your area.

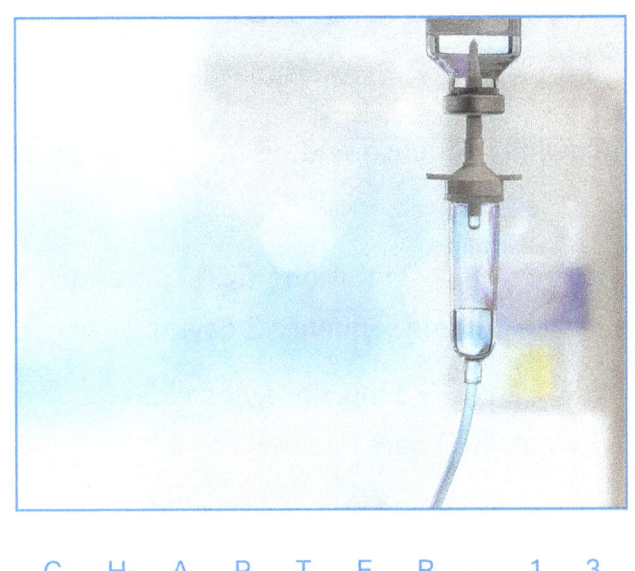

CHAPTER 13

SUPERPOWER #2

HOW I USED ALPHA LIPOIC ACID (ALA) IV THERAPY TO REMOVE TUMMY FLUBBER, DISSOLVE NEUROPATHY, AND GIVE MY BRAIN A BOOST
PLUS TAKE DEEP BREATHS—

I did not see this next thing coming! After years of experimenting with numerous products, I thought I had seen everything, until I worked with sequential infusions of Alpha Lipoic Acid. Before this sequencing, I occasionally tried a single IV and noted that a few more brain cells were "pinging." That would last a day or two; then, I would return to denser brain fog. Then, I tried the following sequence and discovered a serious holy grail.

- WEEK 1 – 2 infusions in 300 mg and each 500 mg sequence 2 days in a row.
- WEEK 2 – 3 infusions, each 500 mg daily, 3 days in a row.
- WEEK 3 – 3 infusions, each 500 mg daily, 3 days in a row.

The results were impressive. My brain is clear continually. I take on mental projects with ease. My feet are generally no longer cold at night, although this is monitored and now treated when my toes feel a little numb or tingly. I lost extra inches off my waist, although it's not a free ticket, as that weight can be regained if diet and exercise are ignored. Two decades of chronic sinus infections have vastly improved, and the constant sinus drainage has significantly diminished. I can once again take deep, refreshing breaths of air.

While ALA is commonly used to cleanse the liver, I found it to be underrated and overlooked considering its ability to metabolize fat throughout my body and the remarkable success I had with neuropathy.

Call to Action

If you frequently experience cold extremities, such as hands and feet, consider researching the benefits of ALA. It is important to take charge of your healthcare and make decisions based on what is right for you.

What's Your WHY for Being Healthy?

> *"The quality of your life is built on the quality of your decisions."*
>
> WESAM FAWZI

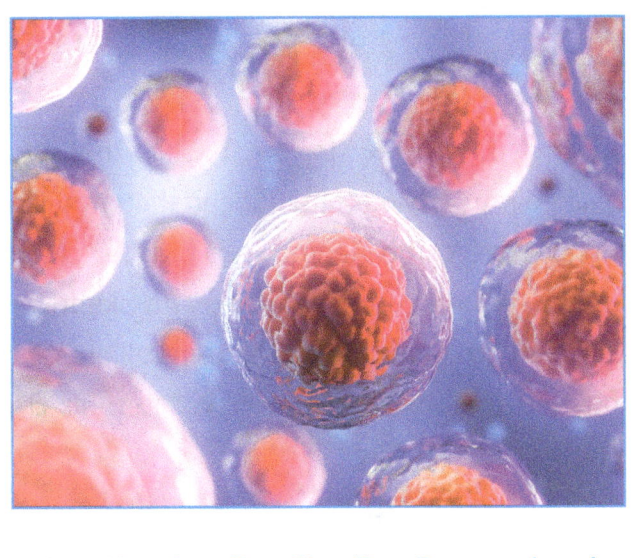

CHAPTER 14

SUPERPOWER #3

HOW I USED STEM CELL THERAPY FOR SIGNIFICANT MEMORY REPAIR, A SERIOUS ENERGY BOOST PLUS ZERO BACK PAIN!

Years ago, Stem Cell Therapy was a controversial topic. The rumors were that stem cells were derived from aborted fetuses, however, I used stem cells that were harvested from my own abdominal fat cells. These were spun out in a centrifuge to extract stem cells and then reintroduced into my bloodstream in an intravenous saline solution. Commercial companies now collect stem cells from mesenchymal (medical signaling cells) extracted post-partum from an umbilical cord. Reputable labs vet sources for the Covid vaccine.

What's Your WHY for Being Healthy?

I became interested in Stem Cell Therapy as I approached my early 60s and noticed that my willpower no longer overcame increasing fatigue. A friend, who is an engineer, conservative, and skeptical, was "volunteered" to participate in a stem cell presentation at a physician's seminar. Three days later, his crippled knees were dancing a jig.

Unfortunately, I contracted cancer during the period between when the FDA pulled experimental stem cell therapy off the market and when it evolved into the protocols offered today. Now, I am back on track in my 70s and feeling a hundred times better than I did in my 60s. The following is an excerpt from a blog I wrote in 2021 after I reinstated stem cell therapy.

> WED 10/21: *Stem Cell - Umbilicus via IV at 10:30 am. Simple procedure. This is my first Stem Cell Therapy since approximately 2012. I was scheduled for Friday but just couldn't wait—I'm sooo excited. The physician implemented a stem cell "push" which is a manual insertion of product via IV with an Ozone IV "chaser."*
>
> THU 10/22: *The nurse mentioned I might experience flu-like symptoms. This morning, I woke up slow and groggy but started to perk*

up after my "normal, get moving" regimen. Ready for work but not with the usual get-go. The "above-mentioned "flu-like symptoms" would be considered a mild healing crisis—as my body focused on repair.

I have to remember to drink more water to facilitate the flush of old cells. This feels similar to the cancer die-off I experienced 3 1/2 years ago, only shorter. I will go low-key for a bit and let my body use its resources to optimize healing. No gym today. The BIG TAKE AWAY this morning is ZERO arthritis in my lower back, which had gradually been worsening until I realized that I hadn't vacuumed in 3 months to avoid the pain.

THU 10/22 LATER: *This is the end of Day 2, and I am definitely having a bit of a "healing crisis" in that I ran in low gear for work all day. Home by 6:30 pm after picking up the makings for soup. I am craving homemade chicken soup, of all things. It's on the stove.*

FRI 10/23: *It is the end of Day 3, and I am exhausted but maintaining my work schedule, which included a minor landscaping project in the pouring rain. Jeeze. Such an endeavor in my "weakening 60s" before I became really ill with cancer would have resulted in pneumonia. Not so today, so I'm not complaining! After so many years of feeling run down with cancer and heart disease, I am thrilled with my NEW NORMAL.*

WIN COLUMN

Mine is another successful Stem Cell Therapy. My physician cautioned me that my results would extend over several months and that I might not feel a difference immediately. The results, however, were immediate and substantial.

I am past the fatigue; my immune system is noticeably amped. There is zero pain in my lower back and neck. Stem Cell Therapy, combined with an additional Ozone IV drip, likely provided an overall oxygen boost.

Call to Action

Ask yourself this question: What should I do to have a new and better "normal"? Now, go and do it!

CHAPTER 15

SUPERPOWER #4

HOW I USED EXOSOME IV THERAPY FOR SIGNIFICANT MEMORY REPAIR, ANOTHER SERIOUS ENERGY BOOST AND ACHIEVED ZERO BACK PAIN—

My success with Stem Cell Therapy led me to work with Exosome Therapy for two reasons. As laboratories became more adept at manufacturing exosomes, the cost to patients finally began to moderate (more than stem cells). Also, labs were managing the conversion process from stem cells to exosomes in-house before shipping them to physicians. This is typically a 30-day process and means a faster response time once a patient takes exosomes.

Because I work full time, I did not want to be deterred by having "Some-Timers" (a joke among seniors) turn into "Alzheimer's (never a joke). Neither did I desire joint deterioration. I want to be fully engaged because every moment counts as I grow older. Because of the lack of information and the disinformation, I am committed to learning and testing as much as I can to improve our helath legacy.

AGING

As we age, our bodies' mitochondria grow less efficient at cell repair and replacement. Environmental factors, malnutrition, chronic disease, autoimmune disorders, or chronic inflammation can interfere with or "dysregulate" the communication between cells.

WHAT ARE EXOSOMES

Exosomes used in this therapy are derived from Mesenchymal Stem Cells (MSC) and can work with any type of cell in the body to effect repairs. Their function is to increase communication between cells and convey information that directs cells to turn "on" or "off." Exosomes support the immune system, "calm" the immune response, thus reducing inflammation, and instruct cells to return to healthy function. They can prove helpful in combating chronic inflammation, autoimmune disorders, fibromyalgia, Lyme Disease, and other degenerative diseases.

WHO ADMINISTERS EXOSOME THERAPY?

A physician on an outpatient basis.

TREATMENT

5 cc of Exomes was divided into five applications, then I proceeded as follows:

- STEP 1: The vial is thawed by rolling it between your hands.
- STEP 2: Separate 1 cc for application and administer it into the back of the nasal passage for optimal brain barrier transfer. Check and write down the time.
- STEP 3: Place 1 cc in the dropper; lie with head tilted back and release into the back of the nasal passage.
- STEP 4: Add saline solution to 4 cc and infuse intravenously.
- STEP 5: Prepare and apply Ozone with terpene (biosynthetic building blocks) IV.

- **STEP 6:** One hour after the first nasal application, administer the second 0.25 cc to the back of the nasal passage.
- **STEP 7:** Repeat Step 6.
- **STEP 8:** Repeat Step 7.

IMMEDIATE PHYSICAL REACTION

DAY 1: Morning: One hour after Step 1, my extremities became very cold. I wrapped up in a blanket and rested throughout the rest of the therapy (until 1:30 pm.) I did notice a slight increase in mental clarity that afternoon, but it was still low-key.

DAY 2: I was told to "chill out." The next day was like cruising in low gear—a steady go with the flow was still in low gear 12 hours later. Mentally productive with slightly improved concentration, and I was able to focus on this blog.

DAY 3: This is still another low-gear day, but with steady energy and good concentration.

DAY 8: Still another low-gear day but with steady energy. My olfactory senses have just kicked in, and I have noticed that odors smell stronger, an indicator that it is working on the smell center in my brain, and hopefully, in other areas. My primary reason for trying this therapy was to determine if we could enhance osmotic access through the blood-brain barrier, thereby optimizing cognitive function.

DAY 12: *I was concerned that I wouldn't get arthritic relief, but I'm relieved to know that my lower back is no longer stiff.*

DAY 90: *Overall, I felt better. My skin had noticeably improved, which was interesting. I had an adverse reaction to the first COVID shot, which seemed to lower my pretty robust immune system, and I had bacterial pneumonia for two weeks. My heart had weakened significantly by my last MENLA SCAN (a whole-body evaluation).*

COMPARISON TO STEM CELL THERAPY 6 MONTHS AGO

- I initiated Stem Cell Therapy, in part, for heart repair and to heal arthritis pain in my lower back. That pain disappeared in approximately 12 hours.

- Exosome Therapy took about 10-12 days to begin low back relief. I was told that everyone responds differently and that exosome results are more evident around the third month.

- I experienced mild fatigue for about two weeks following Stem Cell treatment and Exosome Therapy. I experienced marked improvement with both therapies. I am more active and productive later in the evenings. This is HUGE! I have experienced improved mental function. My skin improved significantly with the exosomes, but again, the amount (15 billion) allowed more healing. I had been struggling to improve my immune system after cancer, and both therapies were beneficial.

CONCLUSION

I had planned to do another round of Exosomes, but because my heart took a hit in the past several weeks, I decided to repeat Stem Cell Therapy because it is said to prioritize the heart and lungs.

Call to Action

I believe that Stem Cell and Exosome Therapy are key to senior health as we age, especially in the way they help offset mitochondrial decline. Now is the time to prepare for the future and learn about these therapies, as well as where to find a practitioner near you.

> *"Exosome Therapy was faster acting for me than Stem Cell Therapy and more economical."*
>
> CAROL VAN LUIK

CHAPTER 16

GOING OFF THE RAILS

IMPROVED O^2 DELIVERY BROUGHT REPAIR TO MY WEAKENED HEART MUSCLE AND IRREGULAR HEARTBEAT

Years ago, my physician mentioned that when a person arrives at an Emergency Room with heart issues, the initial response is administering a mineral IV. Do older people become mineral deficient? Backtrack to blocked microcirculation; a couple of things can happen when capillaries to and in the heart become compromised.

- Vascular blockage can prevent minerals that the heart muscle requires from reaching their destination. This can prevent the necessary muscles from clenching and releasing correctly.
- Vascular blockage can prevent the heart's mini-brain—about 40,000 dendrites—from receiving the oxygen and nutrition necessary to orchestrate a proper heartbeat.
- Vascular blockage (plaque) can stiffen blood vessels, causing the heart to beat faster to deliver necessary oxygen and nutrition to the heart muscle.

I have always been fascinated when my friends come back from heart surgery to share the cardiologist's efforts to "roto-rooter" some large blood vessel. I have never heard of any discussion about checking small vessels, which account for 90 to 95% of all circulation. Does anyone else find that concerning?

- I do have to supplement with trace minerals and vitamins, including Potassium, Calcium, and Magnesium, for my heartbeat. Additionally, I supplement K2 and D3 to support calcium uptake in my muscles.

- Acetyl-L-Carnitine, Pantothenic Acid, and Aminos have been very helpful in strengthening my heartbeat, that is to say, a stronger "thub-lub." This I can actually track with a before and after EKG.

Call to Action

Maintaining healthy microcirculation is crucial for vibrant health at all ages. Consider body cleansing now and avoid the train wreck that we commonly refer to as heart disease, which can lead to heart failure. Be intentional. Learn how to use an Oximeter to monitor oxygen absorption. During my sick years, my Oximeter readings were 92-93%. Ugh. I never thought that it would improve, however, I am now back up to 97-98% and have sustainable energy! A stethoscope can also help you to recognize different heart rates and strengths. When I am deficient in the nutrients mentioned above, my heart does become irregular and cannot sustain a strong beat. A weakened heart can contribute to fatigue as it reduces oxygen delivery.

Maintaining healthy microcirculation is crucial for vibrant health at all ages.

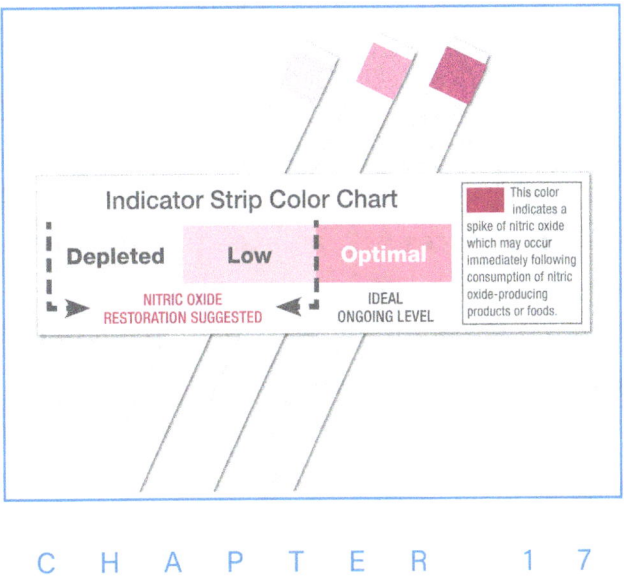

CHAPTER 17

WIPE OUT!

THE ROLE OF OXYGEN UPTAKE—
THE O²/NITRIC OXIDE CONNECTION
AND HEALING BLOOD VESSELS
(VERSUS CLEANING)

If you were not fully attentive to earlier conversations, the human body has about 20,000 miles of blood vessels. 90-95% is only about one cell wide. Thus, it is easy to clog tiny blood vessels. Nevertheless, they can also be cleaned out.

The buildup of plaque, minerals, and other debris in blood vessels degrades circulation, depriving the blood vessel lining, known as the glycocalyx, of the oxygen and nutrients it needs. When compromised, this lining can no longer perform other essential duties. For example, glycocalyx produces B12, an essential factor in mental health. Blood vessels also produce nitric oxide, an important facilitator of oxygen uptake into all cells in the body. This is of paramount importance. Oxygen is essential for mitochondria to orchestrate cellular repair and replacement.

I have used a product called Endocalyx® for several years to repair the vascular lining. After cleansing my circulatory system with Ozone Therapy, I noticed the "uptake" was faster, and now I can skip the afternoon dose. All products work more effectively when the blood vessels are maintained to optimize absorption.

If I become chronically fatigued, I use Nitric Oxide Test Strips (Humann) to check my Nitric Oxide levels and adjust accordingly. Nitric Oxide facilitates oxygen uptake into the cells, which is why it is so important. Low Nitric Oxide can definitely contribute to fatigue. I used Nitric Oxide sublingual tablets in the past, but with my currently cleaner blood vessels and better absorption, I can get excellent results with spinach salads and/or fresh leafy greens, celery, and beets.

Afternoon naps are a thing of the past, and I have more time to enjoy life.

Call to Action

Purchase Nitric Oxide Indicator Strips (Humann) to test your Nitric Oxide levels. It's a great tool, especially if you deal with much fatigue. Initially, I thought only "old people" would test "low" (white or light pink), so I was surprised that even children and young adults tested low. Nobody eats enough salads! You can purchase beet pills, but real beets and spinach are magical foods that make my Nitric Oxide Indicator Strips a bright HOT PINK now that my blood vessels are cleaned up—a good reflection of oxygen uptake and absorption. Fit them into your diet often. It's worth the effort!

Maintaining healthy microcirculation is crucial for vibrant health at all ages.

CHAPTER 18

OZONE IV THERAPY

I would have loved to have known about Ozone Therapy in my 50s when my stress was "maxed out." Stress affected my work productivity, and the soul-sucking fatigue negatively impacted my ability to be 100% with my family.

Ozone Therapy has been used in Europe for over 50 years and practiced in the U.S. since the 1980s. Dr. Frank Shallenberger, President of AAOT, is also a founding member of the International Scientific Committee on Ozone Therapy (ISO3). The following is taken directly from The American Academy of Ozone Therapy literature:

Ozone Therapy utilizes medical-grade ozone, a highly active form of pure oxygen, to initiate a curative process in the body. The body has the potential to renew and regenerate itself. When it becomes sick, it is because this potential has become blocked. The reactive properties of ozone stimulate the body to remove many of these impediments, allowing the body to do what it does best ... heal itself.

OZONE THERAPY HELPS TREAT VARIOUS DISEASES

- *It activates the immune system.*
- *It improves the cellular utilization of oxygen, which reduces ischemia (inadequate blood supply) in cardiovascular diseases and many of the infirmities of aging.*
- *It releases growth factors that stimulate damaged joints and degenerative discs to regenerate.*
- *It can dramatically reduce and even eliminate many causes of chronic pain through its action on pain receptors.*

Published papers have demonstrated the healing effect of Ozone Therapy on interstitial cystitis, chronic hepatitis, herpes, dental infections, diabetes, and macular degeneration.

Call to Action

This is the Holy Grail for your health! Check AAOT.us for an Ozone Therapy practitioner in your area.

***Your health is your responsibility.
Be informed and proactive—ultimately, you are responsible for your own care.***

CHAPTER 19

ALPHA LIPOIC ACID IV THERAPY

My family physician warned me about high cholesterol but countered it with, "Your good cholesterol numbers were higher, so you should be okay." Another physician commented that fat, good or bad, will stick … somewhere. Eww. Oh, I know where!

Alpha-Lipoic Acid is an essential nutrient for fat metabolism (Shallenberger, 2022). It is a well-known liver cleanse. When a physician suggested I check out Alpha-Lipoic Acid IVs (ALA), I recalled trying a few infusions, and my brain did perk up … for about a day. Maybe it was time to focus like I had with the Ozone Therapy. I did not anticipate the results obtained by linking ALA IVs together in sequences of 2–3 days.

What's Your WHY for Being Healthy?

DATE	DOSAGE	RESULTS
01.31.24	Alpha Lipoic Acid 475-600mg	Mental Improvement, Better Energy
02.01.24	Alpha Lipoic Acid 475-600mg	Mental Improvement, Better Energy
02.02.24	Alpha Lipoic Acid 475-600mg	Mental Improvement, Better Energy
02.13.24	Alpha Lipoic Acid 475-600mg	Mental Improvement, Better Energy
03.06.24	Alpha Lipoic Acid 475-600mg	No Phlegm, Sinus Infection, Precancerous Skin Reversed
03.07.24	Alpha Lipoic Acid 475-600mg	Healing From Illness & Infections Without Antibiotics
03.08.24	Alpha Lipoic Acid 475-600mg	Healing From Illness & Infections Without Antibiotics
04.09.24	Alpha Lipoic Acid 475-600mg	Healing From Illness & Infections Without Antibiotics
04.12.24	Alpha Lipoic Acid 475-600mg	No Cold Toes At Night; No Neuropathy

By the tenth infusion, I could feel the ALA in the vessels behind my eyes. It felt clean, like there was no more "crust" in my blood vessels. This is a subjective comment, but the results are honest. I now have sustainable daily energy and mental acuity. I was able to stop using antibiotics after fighting what I was told were sinus infections due to allergies for two decades (this fight is not quite over, but much improved). I wonder whether some of that phlegm resulted from brain inflammation draining into sinuses. I have had no more drainage or allergies.

Just when I think I have learned everything ... BAM! My health improves by another notch... really, ten notches. That foot neuropathy was terrifying. First, it is just tingling, then numbness, then you cannot feel your feet, then it is very easy to stumble and fall. This is common for older people along with severe head injuries. I have seen people with mangled and amputated toes in their later years. And I reversed it with eleven ALA IVs? Hmmmm ...

Call to Action

Take your circulation seriously, and the sooner the better. Purchase Nitric Oxide Indicator Strips (available at this website or at Humann) and an Oximeter (found at a drugstore) to learn how to identify your sources of stress, such as low oxygen absorption.

CHAPTER 20

EXOSOMES VS. STEM CELL THERAPY

Ozone Therapy and Alpha-Lipoic Acid IVs were huge game changers. I felt they cleaned out decades of built-up debris, i.e., fat and inflammatory residue, and provided increasingly more oxygen and nutritive access to cells for regeneration. Imagine not vacuuming your home for 70 years.

During this time, I also worked with Stem Cells (Oct 2020) and Exosomes (see list following) because my "Some-Timers" was turning into something more … maybe Alzheimer's? Certainly, the early indications of dementia. That "brain fog" was looking more like cognitive impairment.

EXOSOMES		
KIMERA May 2021	15 Billion	5 cc
ORGANICELL Feb 2022	400 Billion	1-Unit
ED PURE Nov 2022	100 Billion	4.5 cc

Stem cells, derived from the human umbilicus, convert over 30 days into RNA (ribonucleic acid) messengers that travel throughout the body with reproductive information for cells that cannot reproduce correctly. As business would have it, this created two divergent product lines:

STEM CELLS

This is the more expensive treatment, but it also appears to prioritize the heart and brain.

EXOSOMES

This therapy is less expensive and faster-acting since the 30-day conversion is already accounted for. Exosomes operate in a more "shotgun" approach, with no prioritized agenda, so cell repair is first-come, first-served.

When Important Info Is Too Little, Too Late (Almost)

As I am committed to not burdening my children, so I am intentional and diligent about protecting my health. Both Stem Cells and Exosomes work well for me. Currently, I load up about every six months when I can't remember words or concepts. Worth it? Absolutely.

Call to Action

Improving your health requires critical thinking. Be intentional because I promise that the healthcare industry is not looking out for you, and your trust in them having your best interest at heart is misplaced. I say this with the understanding that there are, indeed, good and great physicians. That said, it is imperative that you know your health options, and if you have an alternative inclination, then know which health professionals support your belief system.

Although a less focused therapeutic approach than Stem Cell Therapy, Exosomes are effective at cell repair and more cost-effective if budget is an issue.

CHAPTER 21

EPIPHANIES—COME AND GET 'EM!

EPIPHANY #1—

After my cancer regimen, Ozone Therapy and Alpha-Lipoic Acid IVs were big game changers when it came to healing my body. I feel they cleaned out inflammation and built-up debris. Furthermore, Stem Cell Therapy and Exosomes resulted in a major reset. It's awesome!

EPIPHANY #2—

Much of the health community has missed the importance of vascular health, and they overlook the repercussions of sick blood vessels. They tend to push pills, not solutions. Have you read the disclaimers?

Those alone were enough to prompt me to conduct my own research.

EPIPHANY #3—

Sick blood vessels are for real! They prevent nutrients and oxygen from flowing to cells and can reduce the effectiveness of medicinal products, making them a waste of money.

EPIPHANY #4—

I find IV (intravenous) therapies are more effective than pills because they bypass the digestive tract. **Exception:** If infusion therapies (IVs) are not convenient or readily available, check out Liposomal products that can circumvent digestive enzymes. They are available in both pill and liquid forms, and can be placed under the tongue.

EPIPHANY #5—

A former pharmaceutical representative tacitly agreed with my assertion that manufacturers provide just enough substance in a pill or IV to get you hooked but not enough to heal you. She smiled and said, "Ah, you figured it out." Indeed.

EPIPHANY #6—

According to one physician, the average senior will spend about $240,000 in out-of-pocket health expenses after retirement on healthcare (Dr. Frank Shallenberger, AAOT Annual Meeting, 2024).

Call to Action

Don't wait 'til you break. Now is the time for action!

You can prepare and prevent or repair and repent.

Either way—you must take care of your health.

CHAPTER 22

YOUR HOLY GRAIL

Actually, my first real epiphany occurred in 1971, studying Pre-Med Biology as a Psychology major (S.U.N.Y. Albany, NY). As the professor uploaded an image of "The Female Hormone Cycle" onto the screen, I noticed that the hormonal ups and downs perfectly matched what I know to be my monthly cycle ... and my emotional cycle. Surely, I thought, it couldn't be that basic.

While teaching small women's groups, I cautiously introduced the "Hormone–Emo Concept" to see if other women shared a similar emotional correlation to their monthly cycles. They all started laughing, visibly relieved that they weren't the only ones. The concept later trended as "PMS" (Pre-Menstrual Syndrome) in the mid-1970s.

After a lifetime of business-kids-family-college … and then cancer, I found myself jolted back to the beginning and once again reviewing how the body works. What had I missed? And, what could I have avoided (a.k.a. the "train wreck" in my 60s)?

MY TAKEAWAYS

1. Not to assume what others think is 100% true.
2. Two highly intelligent and highly educated physicians can have radically different, diametrically opposed opinions regarding the same subject.
3. My opinion is valid as long as I have done my homework.

I am glad that I stayed for another chapter in the book of life. It has been tremendously rewarding. Now it's your turn to write your own chapter!

REFERENCES

CHAPTER 1

1. Anand, P., Kunnumakara, A. B., Sundaram, C., Harikumar, K. B., Tharakan, S. T., Lai, O. S., ... & Aggarwal, B. B. (2008). Cancer is a preventable disease that requires major lifestyle changes. Pharmaceutical Research, 25(9), 2097-2116.
2. Lichtenstein, P., Holm, N. V., Verkasalo, P. K., Iliadou, A., Kaprio, J., Koskenvuo, M., ... & Hemminki, K. (2000). Environmental and heritable factors in the causation of cancer—analyses of cohorts of twins from Sweden, Denmark, and Finland. New England Journal of Medicine, 343(2), 78-85.
3. American Cancer Society. (2024). Breast Cancer Facts & Figures 2024. Retrieved from https://www.cancer.org
4. Barnard, N. D., Bush, A. I., Ceccarelli, A., Cooper, J., de Jager, C. A., Erickson, K. I., ... & Wang, Y. (2014). Dietary and lifestyle guidelines for the prevention of Alzheimer's disease. Neurobiology of Aging, 35(2), S74-S78.
5. Ornish, D., Magbanua, M. J. M., Weidner, G., Weinberg, V., Kemp, C., Green, C., ... & Carroll, P. R. (2005). Changes in prostate gene expression in men undergoing an intensive nutrition and lifestyle intervention. Proceedings of the National Academy of Sciences, 105(24), 8369-8374.
6. Feinberg, A. P. (2007). Epigenetics at the epicenter of modern medicine. JAMA, 299(11), 1345-1350.

CHAPTER 2

1. Bloom, D. E., Cafiero, E. T., Jané-Llopis, E., Abrahams-Gessel, S., Bloom, L. R., Fathima, S., ... & Weiss, J. (2011). The Global Economic Burden of Noncommunicable Diseases. Geneva: World Economic Forum.
2. Celermajer, D. S., Chow, C. K., Marijon, E., Anstey, N. M., & Woo, K. S. (2012). Cardiovascular Disease in the Developing World: Prevalence, Patterns, and the Potential of Early Disease Detection. Journal of the American College of Cardiology, 60(14), 1207-1216.

3. Rognoni, A., Cavallini, C., & Venerando, A. (2016). Microcirculation and Cardiovascular Disease the Forgotten Circulation. Minerva Medica, 107(4), 265-279.
4. Bocci, V. (2006). Scientific and Medical Aspects of Ozone Therapy. State of the Art. Archives of Medical Research, 37(4), 425-435.
5. Microvascular Research. (2018). Endocalyx Product Study on Vascular Health. Microvascular Research Journal.

CHAPTER 3

1. Smith, T. J. (2000). Evidence-Based Cancer Care and the Wise Oncologist. Journal of Clinical Oncology, 18(23), 4089-4091.
2. Haller, D. G., Glick, J. H., & Gelber, R. D. (2010). Chemotherapy: Toxicities. In Cancer: Principles & Practice of Oncology.
3. American Cancer Society. (2023). Cost of Cancer Treatment. Retrieved from https://www.cancer.org.
4. Pollitz, K., Cox, C., Lucia, K., & Keith, K. (2016). Understanding the Medical Loss Ratio. Health Affairs.
5. Hibbard, J. H., Stockard, J., Mahoney, E. R., & Tusler, M. (2004). Development of the Patient Activation Measure (PAM): Conceptualizing and Measuring Activation in Patients and Consumers. Health Services Research, 39(4 Pt 1), 1005-1026.
6. Ornish, D., Brown, S. E., Scherwitz, L. W., Billings, J. H., Armstrong, W. T., Ports, T. A., ... & Brand, R. J. (1990). Can Lifestyle Changes Reverse Coronary Heart Disease? The Lifestyle Heart Trial. The Lancet, 336(8708), 129-133.

CHAPTER 4

1. Sies, H. (1997). Oxidative Stress: Oxidants and Antioxidants. Experimental Physiology, 82(2), 291-295.
2. Nimse, S. B., & Pal, D. (2015). Free Radicals, Natural Antioxidants, and Their Reaction Mechanisms. RSC Advances, 5(35), 27986-28006.
3. Luscher, T. F. (1990). The Endothelium in Health and Disease. Springer-Verlag.
4. Packer, L. (1998). Alpha-Lipoic Acid as a Biological Antioxidant. Free Radical Biology and Medicine, 19(2), 227-250.
5. Bocci, V. (2006). Scientific And Medical Aspects of Ozone Therapy. State of the Art. Archives of Medical Research, 37(4), 425-435.

References

CHAPTER 5

1. McEwen, B. S. (1998). Protective and Damaging Effects of Stress Mediators. New England Journal of Medicine, 338(3), 171-179.
2. Popkin, B. M., D'Anci, K. E., & Rosenberg, I. H. (2010). Water, Hydration, and Health. Nutrition Reviews, 68(8), 439-458.
3. Celermajer, D. S., Chow, C. K., Marijon, E., Anstey, N. M., & Woo, K. S. (2012). Cardiovascular Disease in The Developing World: Prevalence, Patterns, and The Potential Of Early Disease Detection. Journal of the American College of Cardiology, 60(14), 1207-1216.
4. Booth, F. W., Roberts, C. K., & Laye, M. J. (2012). Lack Of Exercise Is a Major Cause of Chronic Diseases. Comprehensive Physiology, 2(2), 1143-1211.
5. Armstrong, L. E., Johnson, E. C., Munoz, C. X., Swokla, B., Le Bellego, L., Jimenez, L., & Casa, D. J. (2016). Hydration Biomarkers and Dietary Fluid Consumption of Women. Journal of the Academy of Nutrition and Dietetics, 116(5), 739-758.
6. Warburton, D. E., Nicol, C. W., & Bredin, S. S. (2006). Health Benefits of Physical Activity: The Evidence. CMAJ, 174(6), 801-809.

CHAPTER 6

1. McEwen, B. S. (1998). Protective and Damaging Effects of Stress Mediators. New England Journal of Medicine, 338(3), 171-179.
2. Chrousos, G. P. (2009). Stress and Disorders of the Stress System. Nature Reviews Endocrinology, 5(7), 374-381.
3. Hotamisligil, G. S. (2006). Inflammation and Metabolic Disorders. Nature, 444(7121), 860-867.
4. Kudielka, B. M., & Kirschbaum, C. (2005). Sex Differences in HPA Axis Responses to Stress: A Review. Biological Psychology, 69(1), 113-132.
5. Bocci, V. (2006). Scientific and Medical Aspects of Ozone Therapy. State of the Art. Archives of Medical Research, 37(4), 425-435.

CHAPTER 7

1. Ross, R. (1999). Atherosclerosis—An Inflammatory Disease. New England Journal of Medicine, 340(2), 115-126.
2. Libby, P. (2002). Inflammation in Atherosclerosis. Nature, 420(6917), 868-874.
3. Packer, L. (1998). Alpha-Lipoic Acid as a Biological Antioxidant. Free Radical Biology and Medicine, 19(2), 227-250.
4. Bocci, V. (2006). Scientific and Medical Aspects of Ozone Therapy. State of the Art. Archives of Medical Research, 37(4), 425-435.

CHAPTER 8

1. Meyer, J. H., & Castell, D. O. (1981). Gastric and Intestinal Digestion. Handbook of Physiology.
2. Caplan, A. I. (1991). Mesenchymal Stem Cells. Journal of Orthopedic Research, 9(5), 641-650.
3. Kirschbaum, C., Pirke, K. M., & Hellhammer, D. H. (1999). Adrenocortical and Subjective Responses to Stress in Healthy Elderly Males. Journal of Psychosomatic Research, 46(2), 113-124.
4. Lobo, R. A. (2008). Menopause and Aging. The Obstetrician & Gynecologist, 10(4), 235-242.

CHAPTER 9

5. Berwick, D. M. (2009). What "Patient-Centered" Should Mean: Confessions of an Extremist. Health Affairs, 28(4), w555-w565.
6. Genuis, S. J. (2011). Elimination of Persistent Toxicants from The Human Body. Human & Experimental Toxicology, 30(1), 3-18.
7. Packer, L. (1998). Alpha-Lipoic Acid as a Biological Antioxidant. Free Radical Biology and Medicine, 19(2), 227-250.
8. Bocci, V. (2006). Scientific and Medical Aspects of Ozone Therapy. State of the Art. Archives of Medical Research, 37(4), 425-435.

References

CHAPTER 10

1. Bocci, V. (2006). Scientific and Medical Aspects of Ozone Therapy. State of the Art. Archives of Medical Research, 37(4), 425-435.
2. Fitzgerald, R. K., & Broussard, J. (2010). Legal and Ethical Issues in Complementary and Alternative Medicine. Journal of Legal Medicine, 31(1), 1-19.

CHAPTER 11

1. Richardson, M. A., Sanders, T., Palmer, J. L., Greisinger, A., & Singletary, S. E. (2004). Complementary/Alternative Medicine Use in A Comprehensive Cancer Center and The Implications For Oncology. Journal of Clinical Oncology, 18(13), 2505-2514.
2. Bocci, V. (2006). Scientific and Medical Aspects of Ozone Therapy. State of the Art. Archives of Medical Research, 37(4), 425-435.

CHAPTER 12

1. Shallenberger, F., M.D., H.M.D. (2017). The Ozone Miracle: How You Can Harness The Power of Oxygen To Keep You And Your Family Healthy.

CHAPTER 22

1. Shallenberger, F., M.D., H.M.D. (2006, 2022). Bursting With Energy: The Breakthrough Method to Renew Youthful Energy and Restore Health.

> *"If we knew what we were doing, it wouldn't be called research."*
>
> ALBERT EINSTEIN

IT'S PERSONAL

MEET CAROL VAN LUIK

I was on a quest in my 50s to avoid the stereotypical age-related illness—you know, "planning ahead." After all, the health issues my older friends were experiencing were daunting. At the time, I had a great family physician who even held meetings for patients. Her passion was research and her patients. We were her subjects, I suspect, and very fortunate to learn right along with her.

What really got my attention was that she was successfully curing HIV patients on the QT to avoid recrimination. To her, I think that HIV was just another "bug," and you kill bugs by changing their biome so they can't proliferate.

She was so intelligent and refreshing. When she passed unexpectedly, I never really found another physician who cared to such a degree and could connect the dots. Her influence on me was profound, and her "Kill the Bug & Change the Biome" approach was key to my healing from cancer.

In my 50s, my only identified health issue was "Insulin Resistance." This was characterized by getting tired after meals, constant hunger, and "middle-age weight gain," which we have all been told is normal, so I wasn't too concerned. I believed I was invincible. I wish someone had mentioned how this "little issue" grows into the monster we call **DIABETES** and is the precursor to SO **MUCH MORE**. In fact, some of the medical community consider Alzheimer's to be Type 3 Diabetes. Gradually, my health became compromised until I faced **CANCER** and a significant **COGNITIVE DECLINE** in my mid-60s.

If you are told you have insulin resistance, it should resonate in your head as **INSULIN RESISTANCE** carrying a **BIG RED FLAG** because it is the beginning of the slow decline we call **AGING**. The cool thing now is that we know how to clean "gunk" off things like insulin receptors in the bloodstream and other parts of the body to prevent many common diseases.

I had to refinance my home to heal from cancer and then repair my body. Every nutraceutical purchase seemed to be a single substance with a beginning price of $50.00 for a 30-day supply. After trying a gazillion pills and therapies, I feel that I have gained a solid understanding of what works and what doesn't, and I wish to share this information with others who, like me, are seeking answers.

PURPOSE OF CLARITY MEDICINE

TO TELL THE TRUTH

The purpose of Clarity Medicine is to provide **CLARITY** for our clients! Answers to your questions and empowerment to take the helm of your health journey and steer it in the direction of recovery, longevity, and vitality.

TO EDUCATE

Clarity Medicine was created to debunk the "Aging Myth" and present viable alternatives to preventing and healing illness as we segue through our 50s, 60s, and 70s. Its purpose is to educate from a patient's perspective via books, videos, and a curated list of nutraceuticals and therapies that have proven to be effective.

TO PROVIDE HELP

During my healing journey, it seemed that every supplement I purchased started at $50.00-$100.00, and you were meant to take them perpetually. When I gathered all the things I needed to support my health and healing, the pill count and price tag were not sustainable. My highest priority was to develop something I could take that was effective and affordable. My health was vital to me, and I was on a mission to give my body what it needed. Now, I am passionate about making these nutritional combinations available to others. Only the best ingredients that proved to be repeatedly effective are part of our formula. I vowed I would make them affordable so everyone could have access to good health. We are proud to announce our flagship product— *Alpha* **XTRA**™.

About Carol Van Luik and Clarity Medicine

OUR FLAGSHIP PRODUCT: *Alpha* **XTRA**™

I learned what supplements I needed to "maintenance" my vascular system and make a way for oxygen and nutrients to get where they needed to go. But there were so many things to take; it was overwhelming and expensive. There had to be an easier way to get what I needed. So, using the key elements I use daily for maintenance, I searched out pharmaceutical-grade ingredients and consolidated them so you don't have to purchase each supplement separately.

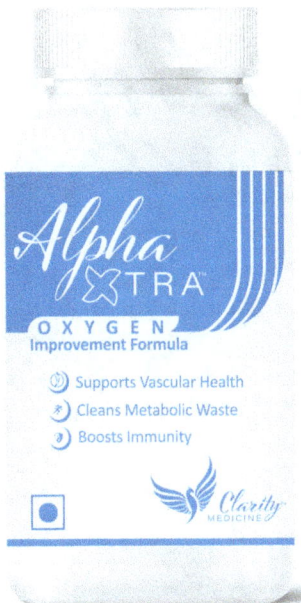

While I never imagined going into manufacturing in my 70s, I am proud to present *Alpha* **XTRA**™ — the foundational formula I use to maintain my vascular health, cognitive clarity, and energy.

CLARITYMEDICINE.COM

What's Your WHY for Being Healthy?

CLARITYMEDICINE.COM

www.ingramcontent.com/pod-product-compliance
Lightning Source LLC
LaVergne TN
LVHW021601070426
835507LV00015B/1899